The
Half Circle

Munia Khan

ISBN 978-1-953223-01-2 (paperback)

Copyright © 2020 by Munia Khan

All rights reserved. No part of this publication may be reproduced, distributed, or transmitted in any form or by any means, including photocopying, recording, or other electronic or mechanical methods without the prior written permission of the publisher. For permission requests, solicit the publisher via the address below.

Rushmore Press LLC
1 800 460 9188
www.rushmorepress.com

Printed in the United States of America

Contents

Preface 7
Acknowledgements 9

Poetry

Before Hail Melts Away 13
Invisible Sign 13
Amur Leopard 13
Predicted 14
Last Hours 14
Mystery 15
Pangolins 15
Do We Need To? 16
Domestic Violence 16
Want 16
River 16
In Memory of Nursery Rhymes 17
Yemen 17
Black Rhinos 18
Earthly Shell 19
Spring 19
These Days 19
Gorilla 20
Contentedness 20
Dhole 20
Forfeit 21
Limitations 21
Left 22

Cruel	22
Poets	22
Own Moments	23
Through the Vulture's flight	23
Ten More	24
Earth	24
V Shaped	25
Simplicity	25
Whales	25
At 3a.m.	26
Fate's Goodbye	26
Black-footed Ferret	28
Proof	28
Dusty Sins	28
Wired	29
The Collusion	30
Sea Turtles	30
Inflated	31
The Chapters of Never	31
Waiting	32
Just A Virus	32
Avarice	34
Saola	34
Pranks	35
Vaquita	36
Gap	36
Murdstone, the RoboCop Teacher	37

Haiku

132 Haiku	41
18 Haiku For My Scottish Friends	67

Thoughts to Ponder	70

Story

Still Remains	75
Another World	81
Elinóra's Judgment	83
Vacation of Innocence	88
Meet Me at Sunset in Vlora	94
Never Far Away	102
Unsheltered	107
The Half Circle	112

PREFACE

I have always been a positive person, that's why I love to be filled with hope. I know it's hard to find colorful colors in the dark, yet we can wait for the blackness to go away. I have written this book with a positive intention to highlight many different things in our lives, viewing from both sides of the curtain. Whether there is a promising light or a depressing murkiness behind the curtain – we have no choice but to deal with it. Through the fictional stories here I've expressed my inner ideas and other feelings about what I see or know or perhaps have experienced.

    I consider myself as an eternal novice in writing the Japanese poetry form called 'Haiku'. In this collection I've presented some of my Haiku written from 2015 till now. The rest of the other verses have come straight from a perplexed mind of the vigilant poet me- a lover of animals, nature and rhyming poetry.

    I believe a half circle, despite being half, does not disappoint us - the half circle of rainbow is a complete form of heavenly creation which contains seven glorious colors bringing joy to our lives. Also a new moon, gradually turns into a half circle before it reaches the full phase, spreading us hope of fulfillment for future.

    I hope my readers will appreciate my simple effort of creating 'The Half Circle' with seven colours of my heart....

Munia Khan
Dhaka, Bangladesh
Sunday, May 31, 2020

Acknowledgements

I'd like to dedicate this collection to my very dear brother Enamul Haque, the Former Senior Business Process Manager at Microsoft who is the very talented author of the books "Digital Transformation Through Cloud Computing" and "Jano".

Also my special dedication goes to my one and only sister Fauzia Haque who has been my inspiration throughout my life with her incredible wit and humor and poetic talent.

My thanks and gratitude I send to all my wonderful author/poet/artist friends from around the world for their unconditional support and encouragement. I extend my gratefulness also to all those people on earth, my amazing readers, who love and appreciate my simple work of writing.

POETRY

Before Hail Melts Away

We need to use the rain water before hail melts away
Hours we have to count before the end of the day
But how can we save the light after the dark
When flickers of flame fade in a moment's spark?

Invisible Sign

Who's going to cross the border
When a land suffers from 'human disorder'
Under the bunk bed, into the cave
All mute men there ready to rave
Talking mouth: sealed, mission fulfilled
Not much, only a few million killed!
Who's going to read the invisible sign
When a world undefined defines things fine

Amur Leopard

Is it a curse having lovely fur?
Great skin of distinction
Will it be just a blur?
Think of their extinction
Rosettes: their exquisite black spots
Widely spaced on thick white or cream
They're the fastest, daring hunting shots
Nimble figures gently drink from the stream
To knock our conscience
They won't bang our doors
Like us they're not silly, nonsense
They are the valorous carnivores

Predicted

A time will come
when emotions will be gone
Birds will stop waiting
for the synchronized dawn
Trees will speak louder
than ever before
Truth will return
through a long closed door
All clocks will watch out
for a never ending time
Life will pay expenses
on its own freaking dime

Last Hours

She's there to save him from eternal fire
Touching the light, warm peace of mind they hire
With the labour of love, no coins of desire
In a world unclothed, faith: their only attire
Somehow they know it, they' re fatally aware
Of the triangle within the secret square
Last hours now nearing, changes are phased
As truth is penniless, all lies: purchased!

Mystery

If internet has become the king of a pandemic world,
smart phone is surely the prime minister.
The question remains: who will be the secretary of state for defense?
- yet to be voted 5G itself or a vaccinated AntiVirus?
What about the ministry of home affairs?

By the way, all those homeless Nokias still laughing
ever since the Gates shut off and Bill stepped down
They also said, Timothy was baking apple pie
on 5th October last year
God knows what they mean

Pangolins

How nocturnal they are!
With poor eye sight
can they see their future far?
They use strong tails quite right
as weapons to defend
their scaly bodies.
Some of them spend
good time with buddies
But most of them: solitary
sleeping in burrows underground
They become a spiky ball, scary
by rolling up when enemies are found
But do they know their real foe
who trades their scales from head to toe?
What can we possibly do
to rescue these anteaters?
This trafficked world we shouldn't renew
We shouldn't be the defeaters

Do We Need To?

Puzzles of fire solved by the ashes
while water wonders- how a piece of glass smashes
the rock beneath the starfishes: embraced
Upon the reddened shore lost-footsteps traced
Our memories do we need to remember,
if from the heart all ache we dismember?

Domestic Violence

His abuse makes her an anvil
without spark
Her life becomes a disease and ill
into the dark

Want

You've got what you wanted
Slope of our faith now leaned and slanted
Hate's broken seeds have just been planted
You've got what you wanted

River

Symphony of peace
is the murmuring sound of a river!
With the shimmering water
I feel my limbs' ecstatic quiver

In Memory of Nursery Rhymes

bedless world-
row row rowing their boat
five little monkeys
baa baa black time-
three bags of wool
seem half cotton
gamers' week-
no end of
Solomon Grundy
rock-a-bye baby-
poor Simple Simon
now counting the sheep
puppy love-
Jack and Jill
putting Humpty together
cock a doodle do-
cyber Billy Boy finds the shoe
for Miss Muffet

Yemen

Long ago, they didn't know
how to starve
They never remained thirsty, either.
Only in the holy month,
they stayed without food and water
for many hours
And they loved it

Now they feel like eating
the wounded ants
from an abandoned cookie-jar

They don't want to live
in this southern edge
of the Arabian peninsula
They want a hail storm to come
and rescue them
as they are so parched.
The dryness of the bombshell
makes them more dehydrated
than last summer

The most surprising hit-and-run raids
don't surprise them anymore
They only care about
their choked up throats and lives.
They only want to drink some water
No…no blood, only water

Black Rhinos

Really grey in color
They're angry fight masters
Many of them die
in combat disasters
Being hook-lipped
they feel very proud
Can oxpeckers save their horns
stolen in the crowd?

Earthly Shell

Melodies of laughter will be heard long after
the day you pass by, leaving loved ones sigh
And sad sound of cry before tears gone dry
will make you weep more within the deep core
of your earthly shell where a lone soul dwell

Spring

When the river needs its murmuring sound
Inside my heart the swan-song I've found
The softness of grass beneath my feet
Another holy morning here to greet
Fragrance of spring carried by the bloom
Taking hope in, breaking away from gloom

These Days

Petals: fallen and torn
Child dead inside, unborn
Lovers: loveless, forlorn
Do we need more themes of scorn?
Wooden walkway, milky
Crow's voice: smooth and silky
Faster heartbeats: dicky
Should this world be more tricky?

Gorilla

This is marvelous
They share 95%
of their DNA with us
Their personality: displayed individually
They are fat babes visually
Depth of muddy water
with the sticks they test
With 10-year-old mother gorilla
her off-springs rest
So endangered now
these African apes
One day we'll be missing
their enormous shapes

Contentedness

When your heart with happiness
full to the brink
Just a glass of water will make your day
if you're able to drink
Blessings of life thus we should count
Life-struggles slowly we will surmount

Dhole

The real stunners
The fast runners
Reddish brown beauties
Sometimes beige cuties
I love them in charcoal grey

For hours they chase the prey
What do they do with 40 teeth
When twelve pups look at them
from underneath
They have to just rip open their food
These wild foxy dogs can whistle so good

FORFEIT

Sometimes memories want us to leave
As gambled time plays with cards of forfeit
When grief becomes joy, nothing's there to grieve
Heart fails to recognize it's own life's beat

LIMITATIONS

When we have our teeth,
we are unable to chew without them-
like knowing our mother-tongue,
it's impossible that we don't understand it.
If you are a native English speaker,
you are unable to shut off your sense
of understanding the English language

As long as you have all your healthy teeth,
you are unable to chew with your gum.
Why would you even want to?
It's against nature.
There are many simple things
we, humans will fail to do.
And that is the limitation of being a human,
the most evolved of all creatures

LEFT

...and she left him
after 25 days
she left...
The answer of sadness
was too pale and bleak
to let the questions sparkle
because she left herself behind
to save her own flesh

CRUEL

Cruelty must have a direction
East or south...
North or west...
We hardly know
And when he becomes cruel
He goes upwards
Like a rocket
Aiming the moon

POETS

(I)

We are the creator of words and wonder
We create rainbow out of silver thunder
Lightning comes down slashing our lines
And all glory and praise be the divine's

(II)

Poetry is genderless
But...
To find a poet, look into the solid armour of his poems
To find a poetess, look deep inside the heart of her poetry

Own Moments

Beauty has its own moments to share
its glorious value with the limbs of trees
which know how to provide strength and care
to the wild wound from an unknown breeze

Through the Vulture's flight

Riding on a vulture
flying with its safer wings
May be against my culture
but the security it brings
comforts me to no end
A lifetime I can spend
like this- looking at its prey
which is dead and grey
It doesn't eat
the living
Like we humans do,
deceiving
humanity's norm
Are we worse
than a worm?
Are we?

The flea
knows it best
It can well rest
feeding upon our blood
knowing us better
tasting dusty mud

Ten More

If you water a tree,
it will remember you the whole year through
If you plant a tree, it will remember you forever
And when you cut a tree, the other trees won't curse you
but they will recognize you as a killer
until you plant ten more trees
and water them throughout your life

Earth

The astronauts are talking too much
before landing
Why on earth the people on earth
so demanding
We say-
'Please, give us some space
Go back to outer space'
They said-
'We will, but first need to study the sun'
cause the test in the world is forever undone

V Shaped

Your heart is not round
It is kind of V shaped
V for Victory
You can only win with your heart

Simplicity

Where will we look for a glistening path
led by the fallen stars from blue aftermath?
Will the owl stop fearing its own hooting
of sadness filled with sound polluting?
Where will we find a healing story
of a soothing lake under sunlight glory?
Will the swans float with white feathers weak
giving solace of peace to a wild moor: bleak?

Whales

Look at those whales
Fin, right and blue
These legends of sea-tales
have really no clue
about how they are disappearing
when to the sea they're so endearing

At 3a.m.

While the game was on point
Mozzies sat on my palm's joint
Instead of slapping
I chose clapping
having them all dead
Now I'm relaxed in bed
At 3a.m. I compromise
No Mozzie, but with flies
See, this is me
Never trouble free
But kindness is the key
If it's not harmful for thee

Fate's Goodbye

Covid days
Kind soul prays
Still lockdown
Loving town
New rules start
Be alert
Dawn to dusk
Always mask
What is this
curse or bliss?
Can you tell
if you're well?
Am I sick
like a freak?
May I cry?
Let me try
Few months more

Close the door
Stuck in home
London, Rome
All breathless
Who's deathless?
No one here
Now we fear
Who is next?
Without text
I'm typing
News hyping
Burning bridge(s)
Empty fridge
No where car
All too far
Quarantine
Dying teen
Exhaling
Inhaling
Lockdown mind
Where to find
Medicine?
No vaccine
What else now?
Take a bow
Surrender!
Be tender
to your life
Accept strife!
Ta-ta bye
Sobs and sigh

Black-footed Ferret

They are the prairie dog hunters
Many other rodents their confronters
With cute faces wearing black masks
They enjoy performing clever tasks
Black feet, bank-robber-look not their flaws
They love their skinny body and long claws
Their various sounds: chuckles, hisses, barks
Can't be concealed when this cruel world lurks

Proof

(Seventeen years ago)
Ever since my father passed away,
I had begun to feel ageless
Because I got the proof -
'souls are eternal'

Dusty Sins

Is there a curtain to hide your guilt
When dark dust of sins so strongly built
Upon the burnished bronze window frame
Of your life: alive through a dead white fame

WIRED

Too many secrets to keep
Sharks: worn out
digging the ocean deep
Submarine days: long gone, over!
Drunken leaders hang on to hangover
For girls: summer time pullover
For men: sundress in October
Is this season disorderly?
Nope, but all things: set in orderly
Who's going to waste our time anyway?
When we walk in the clouds leaving the sunny way?

No matter where we live
in a city: dirty or pretty
What are we today
without electricity?
We are nothing
without a wire or a cord
Without slicing apple or berry
what can we afford?
But without a charger
we can get larger
than a swollen battery
As we're overcharged with flattery
already…
Are you ready?
To be charged with us
during this time: grievous?
Then don't be wireless
But stay desireless!

The Collusion

Am I the delusion for all illusion?
Find me a solution for the conclusion
Why confusion about the collusion
Have a sort-out of the fusion, soul-pollution

Sea Turtles

Not everyone of them
Having a hard, bony shell
Leatherback, the largest gem
Flexible enough to dwell
With the smallest Hawksbill
Who fights predators still
They paddle away
Many miles a day
These migratory beauties
Love their ecological duties

Kemp's Ridley, Loggerhead
One day will be dead
Olive Ridley and Green
Might swim only on the screen
In Australian water
still living flatbacks
Their threatened selves
don't want to be flashbacks

Inflated

From my own mind
I'm saving my sanity
What will I find
beneath your vanity?
Nothing at all, enough I've tried
Now flatter your inflated pride

The Chapters of Never

It's been so long
Without your song
Of joy and care
When our days of dare
We've left behind
To recall and find
The past so true
Of me, love and you
Things you'd bring
Now around my heart
like a ring
of stone and glory
Not the end of our story
It will go on forever
With the chapters of never
Never-ending loves
Of lovers like doves
What a wonder of splendor
To find your surrender
In memory we swayed
becoming one
as we were made

Waiting

When the ocean stays in peace
she is drawn to its simplicity
wondering how inconceivably
these roaring waves are able to save
a little serenity in her restive heart

She doesn't wish to go away
from this shadowy beach
as the roughness of the sand she feels smoother
than the palm of her own hand
She longs to wait here
right here on this sandy seashore
to find out how far
this simple sea could take her
with the restful flight of its vastness

Just A Virus

Everything depends on how you feel
Whether you bend down
or straight on knees you kneel

You sleep without a bed
or if you need a pillow
nightmares care not,
making you a weeping willow

Doesn't matter
if you are free or stuck
when you're okay
with your aching stomach

On a broken chair
if you can sit,
your legs will relax
having a seat
If you feel right
being jailed in your home,
who's going to scare you
off New York or Rome?

If you get mad at yourself
being too sad
This crazy world
will make you feel glad
by allowing your jaw
to drop over and over
as everything matters
is just a virus, moreover!

If the pain of death
can be bravely endured
You'll feel fine
with the sickness: uncured
If you count the blessing
that today you're alive,
who cares if one day
you fail to survive

Everything depends on how you feel
Whether you're jobless
or paying the bill

Avarice

People think about the division of water
All those meetings
regarding the water rights and so on…
They should ponder over how many gallons
they need, to quench their thirsty avarice?
They need to find some pure water first
to wash the dirt off their filthy political minds

Saola

Tiny sweet tails with three stripes
They are the Asian unicorns
The rarest of all types
of bovids with spindle horns
In front of camera they hardly appear
This photographic world to them unclear

Pranks

This world is full of drunken pranks
Truth-seekers are in the lowest ranks
Here gamer boy is the most bemused lad
God-father forgets his own loving dad
The most melodious lady now the Gaga
Trilogies are everywhere labeled as 'Saga'
Duck becomes Donald, president plays a trump
Muslim girls are busy creating 'hump'
Suffocated doctors, in patient's throat a lump
Off the skyscraper men are to jump
Playing cards now are in need of the dice
The king has to obey the joker's advice
Skin and hair modified with inks and dyes
Who's gonna identify when someone dies?
People: despondent with their original gender
To defend nature who's the defender?
Into the waterless pool, the diver dives
Under the dreamy shade, nightmare survives
Walls are all twisted, war means the mercy
Debates can cause no controversy
Robots are humans, as we've become robot
To please our loved ones what have we bought?
Empty seashores save those dead little crabs
While we concentrate on LCD and tabs
We move around the world using our fingers
To falsify the fact reality lingers
How many days a week- seven or eight?
Aren't we all parasites, eating the bait?

Vaquita

How lovely the dark patches on her lips
The large round ring around her eyes
Her robust shaped body nicely flips
Within the oceanic sky she flies
Without beak her rounded head: precious
Into the watery world she's the most gracious
Who's going to shelter the innocent vaquita?
Looks like the sea itself going to eat her

Gap

There are many kinds of gaps in reality -
Age gap between couples
Gap between furnitures
Gap in understanding of math and history
Gap between finishing education and start working
Gap between vehicles on road or in a parking lot
Gap of time span, financial gap, social gap
Gap between two words in a line
Even gap in the middle of mouth and nose
Or perhaps a small gap between front teeth
What kind of a gap is this social distancing?
Is this a gap to make heartless-humans in fear of death?

Murdstone, the RoboCop Teacher

Inside the class rushing in
On the table crushing in
Murdstone, their teacher
He is no preacher
But teaches geometry
Pi his symmetry
With his marker
He wants to be a sparker
Digging the board
Making them bored
He only knows his daughter
The rest are to slaughter
With his arithmetic knife
As they all strife
With his quick explanation
As if he's from a robotic nation
Like a machine he walks
Like RoboCop he talks
They don't like him that's why
They wait for him to say 'bye'

Haiku

(1)
sleepless night—
her mind on the ceiling
a spinning fan

(2)
unknown path—
flight of his pet bird
guiding her

(3)
peeled onions
hiding pain's melancholy
through different tears

(4)
evening window—
his silhouette surrenders
to her shadow

(5)
missing dad…
show me the road
to heaven

(6)
returning home-
a crow mother finds fur
in her empty nest

(7)
brave selfie
with a buffalo
chasing him

(8)
fifty five selfies
mirror
her only partner

(9)
quiet exam hall-
distracted student writes
about teacher's sneeze

(10)
ultrasound room:
the best sound to her ears
her child's heartbeats

(11)
April song -
symphony of hidden moon
drizzling from the clouds

(12)
end of December -
only the migrating birds
can break the distance

(13)
swan feather floats
on moving water-
rippled beauty

(14)
rainy season-
dancing frogs rest
near the murderer's grave

(15)
today's world-
the bombing hides
sound of fireworks

(16)
burnt down home
only ashes and tears
left behind

(17)
wintry time–
beneath the willow tree
a weeping widow

(18)
traffic jam…
even the morning clouds refrain
from pouring down

(19)
passionate night–
unfolded petals
dripping love

(20)
skin cancer–
her beautiful face
now a memory

(21)
supermoon's new night–
the old river breaks
the silver silence

(22)
robotic life–
outside his computer
he lives with xbox

(23)
teardrops…
wish we could count
the pain

(24)
love poem…
his heart with mine
left there beating

(25)
morning dew–
dragonfly's mirrored face
on the grass-blade

(26)
old time returns-
in today's child bride's eyes
tears of a harem slave

(27)
lover's mind-
eating cherries
reminds him of her

(28)
peace of mind –
even dark clouds look like
cotton flowers

(29)
purrfect -
feline love expressed
through her typing

(30)
reducing stress
with or without sleep…
dreams

(31)
distant rainfall…
all those drops
can't hide her tears

(32)
lonely Valentine…
her toe draws a sandy heart
around the pebbles

(33)
bathing…
the caress of my hair
upon the shore

(34)
enjoying architecture…
I wonder if time stands still
with those pillars

(35)
sleeping late-
summer honeymooners
missed the flight

(36)
grammar class…
don't know why
the plural form of sun

(37)
highway-wheelers -
spinners of lifespan
grandpa and dad

(38)
burning question-
the colours of the skin
or the skin of colours?

(39)
graveyard's narrow beds…
only God knows
how they rest

(40)
frozen ache…
she folded
his bloodstained shirt

(41)
narcissism –
with countable hair
his countless selfies

(42)
stony epitaph -
filled with
his own words

(43)
road accident-
she kisses
on his skin's blue patch

(44)
Syrian mother-
sharing with her four sons
her only bread

(45)
auto correction –
while giggling
she typed *Googling*

(46)
Alzheimer's –
the same question
every time

(47)
rainbows-
after the storm rain bows
to colours of joy

(48)
zoo-
life time imprisonment
for innocent beasts

(49)
Internet –
lifelessness
making lives

(50)
this spring collection…
her shoes, bags
and matching masks

(51)
yummy cheese…
the mouse in me
dreams of Jerry

(52)
preparing barfi-
the hours of stirring
tests my patience

(53)
ghostwriter…
still writing about the ghost
behind Corona

(54)
forest…
comforting us in trouble
our green family

(55)
spice girls…
90s' pop band
still spicy

(56)
somnambulist -
he fastens the seatbelt
to sleep in his car

(57)
time for candy -
in her mouth disappearing
cotton or floss?

(58)
broken family…
the child has to choose
either mom or dad

(59)
apple-
just a single bite
enough for Steve

(60)
blackberry or apple
sugar-coated-words
made the juice

(61)
hepatitis B…
now she dreams to be
a sunflower

(62)
firefighter wonders…
ambulance or the fire-truck
should pass first

(63)
the safest place…
in my daughter's lap
her teddy koala

(64)
kleptomaniac…
he wishes he could steal
the CCTV first

(65)
life in ICU -
just her breathing
makes them content

(66)
wildfires…
wish the bird mother could save
her last child

(67)
winter trees–
frozen memories
of the numb war

(68)
politics –
some verbal tics
of poly-tricks

(69)
mental asylum…
his only trusted friend
a black umbrella

(70)
harvesting time–
human labor perspires
on a distant land

(71)
Twilight enigma
propping the slovenly stars:
blue night's stumbling-block

(72)
prison cell-
from a cannibal's stomach
eleven confessions!

(73)
ageing…
it's silver hair
not grey!

(74)
starlit night-
between the twinkles
her dying wish

(75)
coma –
only the movement
of heart

(76)
wounded sparrow -
she opens
the window wider

(77)
freedom -
the heart knows
its limit

(78)
camouflage -
his lipstick and nail painting
drew kids' attention

(79)
art school…
students sketch some money
for an orphan child

(80)
cyber love-
only soullessness
sates their souls

(81)
suicide attempt…
seeing the runaway train
a lump in his throat

(82)
gamers' clan…
so much fun
to kill our friends

(83)
non-veg day…
yet head stuck in Tuesday
thinking it's Thursday

(84)
1st January…
only eleven more months
to end the beginning

(85)
world animal day -
so many pets never changed
their 'birthday suit'

(86)
winter memories…
for additional trembling
dad bought me horror books

(87)
atheism–
between heaven and hell
mind dangles

(88)
siamese twins…
more than mere siblings
forever

(89)
optimism…
just lost the friendship band
not the friend

(90)
dengue fever…
their little son comes alive
only in dreams

(91)
emptiness…
creating life
with pencil and paper

(92)
adolescence…
fretting himself sick over
his new beard

(93)
child labour…
a nine-year-old earns
from his master's boat

(94)
cyber universe…
through fingertips
earth to earth

(95)
homelessness…
those veterans are tired
of the stars

(96)
mango tang…
can they trust the powder
to break their fast?

(97)
designer perfumes…
they don't need a nose
to smell the money

(98)
sleeping -
a torch and DC comics
under the blanket

(99)
smell of burning leaves
takes me to my childhood…
bonfire

(100)
desert mirage…
wish the glistens of sands
could sate his thirst

(101)
chemotherapy...
for the first time in her life
she ignores hair loss

(102)
the safest place...
in my daughter's lap
her teddy koala

(103)
fake smile...
even his gold tooth glitters
18-carat

(104)
her twilight wish...
to become a kite
just to be with the birds

(105)
my daughter's smile...
now I know
what keeps me alive

(106)
climate change -
penguin family at a loss
behind the iceberg

(107)
faith on afterlife…
after chemo she wears hijab
on her hairless head

(108)
IPL toss…
right side of the coin
flipped the prediction wrong

(109)
night-long lament…
her only escort
a hooting owl

(110)
last day at school -
to the national anthem
only lip syncing

(111)
overcast night…
I can only imagine
a full moon

(112)
thirty years later
under the same banyan again…
school reunion

(113)
money laundering…
his dreams of bank vault
locked in prison-vault

(114)
rough sleepers -
only in dreams
they sleep at home

(115)
never alone -
she talks too much
with the mirror

(116)
mother...
the wonder woman
of every child

(117)
heart to heart...
her mind conceives
another poem

(118)
garbage can...
from the nearby rose garden
a crow flies in

(119)
broken window sash...
his aching leg fracture
feels okay now

(120)
sweet lullaby...
an iron maiden song
is enough

(121)
glittering shore...
wish starfish could twinkle
around her feet

(122)
apple store...
every single bite
empties his wallet

(123)
roots...
growing and growing
to be dead one day

(124)
haiku patient...
to doctors he doesn't talk
only shows

(125)
summer rain...
joy of fasting becomes
a rainbow

(126)
stamp book…
my childhood unfolds
with every page

(127)
Bengali new year-
pigeon white and blood red
everyone's attire

(128)
pilot lockdown…
his only runway
now his bed

(129)
all colors suit
her beautiful body-
dragonfly

(130)
chemistry class…
he writes H2O
correcting HBO

(131)
photo journalist…
to freeze a moment
her long jump

(132)
mirage-
she has forbidden him
to drink the sand

18 Haiku For My Scottish Friends

100 pipers…
any chair in the world
takes him to Scotland

Stoddart's work…
the blindness of Hary
keeps our eyes open

dear unicorn…
with or without wings
they love you the same

immortality…
brave Wallace lives through
all patriots

beauty of old course…
god must be
a golfer himself

kirks -
the same God
lives there

Glasgow surgeon…
life pulsating
between fingertips

nostalgia flows
through that serpentine motion -
Watter o Clyde!

her blue eyes…
every blink
the depth of ocean

wanderlust…
I find no elephant
in the elephant house

Granite city…
ocean meets the dawn
with Dee and Don

Ondine dinner…
her dress matches the colour
of minted pea purée

Fortingall Yew -
'age' never matters
for standing strong

thistles -
spring or winter
the emblem shines

language class -
most quines learn faster
than the louns

irn bru -
colour of a redhead
inside the bottle

highland lass –
how to listen to her tune
only Wordsworth knew

battlefield…
wish today's war-world
could be a folk band
(Note: Battlefield Band is a famous musical
group from Scotland founded in 1969)

Thoughts to Ponder

1. Being unfinished doesn't make you incomplete
2. Success is the fruitful appearance of plans to achieve a goal
3. I believe, trees can taste our breath because when we exhale they inhale us
4. Sometimes we need obscurity to clarify the puzzlement of our lives
5. Dream like the way mermaid dreams
6. Colors are the skins of life
7. Our dreams have butterfly wings to fly on- innocently higher as we are the flyer
8. Perhaps the broken breeze can move the torn curtain between past and a present
9. New year is the glittering light to brighten the dream-lined pathway of future
10. New year is the joyous proof of many memorable beginnings
11. The sky is our greatest treasure
12. Life is very beautiful when you are with yourself. Make yourself worth living with
13. The definition of money resides inside the wallet outside of which poverty remains homeless
14. Love never dies, but yes, it can hibernate in eternal coldness
15. We should forgive people before we pardon ourselves
16. This life is a treasure hunt for the afterlife living
17. Simplicity sates our craving for innocence
18. Dreaming with your eyes closed will make your dreams fall asleep. So, dream with your eyes open wide to keep your dreams awake
19. Sit down on the knees of your ego and learn to apologize
20. Sometimes permanent heartaches depend on our temporary emotions.
21. Getting ahead in politics sucks! Getting around it needs a lot of bucks

22. The construction of our heart is very simple if we know the heart anatomy well. But it is the collision of love and hate within it which is complex.
23. There is nothing to discover by covering the uncovered. Find the bare truth within the nakedness.
24. The return of a long lost friend is the revival of glee
25. Don't be worried about losing him or her. Stay careful about losing yourself
26. If we don't put the oil of love in our heart-machine, we will become robots
27. Letting go is utterly agonizing, but we still have to let go
28. We are tired of observing, responding and reacting. Now it is time to step forward- initiating and doing…
29. It doesn't require darkness of mind to think wise
30. If we were memoryless, our pain would be lessen
31. A door can be closed from both sides
32. Even difficulties have difficult time to face the time sometimes
33. We should always stay away from darkness unless we have a torch or any source of light with us; it can be our inner light, if we have much.
34. A lake has beautiful breath fresher than the oxygen I inhale from a polluted city

STORY

Still Remains

It was, he sensed, one of those fairly cool October evenings in England, when his father used to read him story books while his mother was preparing supper. Now dozing in the rocking chair, he felt the little robin family residing next to the tree near his balcony needed to go to sleep. Every evening the light coming from the neighbourhood tennis court made him so vigorously alive. He had been sitting here for the last hour enjoying how the dusk was falling so rapidly only to be conquered by the night. David Ashcroft, a retired man of 67 summers had been a lover of twilight throughout his life. Now his life seemed to have reached its own twilight. Sarah Ashcroft, his beloved wife still dazzled his life with the twinkles of her blue eyes, as if she would remain the brightest star of his life forever.

She was in the kitchen preparing dinner when David realized that these days he was more in love with living in the past than spending time with Sarah. Specially, through his mind he loved to roam around his early childhood days. From one moment to another his memory loved to step back only to rediscover the past. In his mind, today, several times he was in the literature class of 9th grade at high school when he won the writing contest defeating his best friend 'Fox Jim'. He laughed alone thinking about those fun filled days. He used to call his buddy James Dodd 'Fox Jim', as he was the cleverest boy in town, David believed. He couldn't help laughing recalling how Fox Jim, at age 8, taught him how to blow smoke rings with the stolen cigarette from Jim's father's drawer.

Suddenly his mind's journey to his childhood days was interrupted by the most familiar voice in the world asking him- "Dave, aren't you hungry, darling?"

"Yes, I am sweetheart" he replied to his wife with a fragile smile on his chain smoking lips.

Sarah came closer. "I know, you'd love the lamb chops I've cooked tonight. I tried a new recipe", she said about the chops that David brought from the store this morning as she was rubbing her oily hands with the kitchen towel.

"Lamb? When did you buy lamb chops?" David asked surprisingly as he remembered it had been ages since they bought lamb chops last.

"Just this morning you bought it, remember?," Sarah replied winking her left eye to give David the impression that she knew he had a naughty tendency to tease her sometimes by asking strange questions.

"What do you mean? When did I go out today?" David asked raising his eyebrows, and his blood pressure. "I never went to the store today," he confirmed with a shaking fearful voice.

"Oh! Come on, dearest! Stop joking. I'm not in the mood. I'm too hungry to cope with your puzzling joke now," said Sarah.

"Let's have dinner" she said sitting on a 37 year old wooden chair which carried memories from their wedding night.

David felt his sinking heart when he said, "No, I am not jesting! What are you talking about?"

"Are you serious that you cannot remember you went out this morning", Sarah asked in a shrewd way as if she was an attorney cross-examining a mugger who stole her husband's wallet few hours ago.

"No! Honey, Trust me!! I cannot recall anything. I cannot tell where I was this morning." David's voice was at a loss as to what more to say.

He tried to ransack his memory and all he found was he and his father buying a brand new bicycle on his birthday fifty nine years ago.

"Okay. I understand. Now let's eat; I don't want to talk about it" said Sarah. She was in a very sad state of mind and her hunger for food was consumed by her hunger for knowing the mystery of how this morning could become a forgotten time to her husband who had been blessed by a sharp memory throughout his life.

They finished the dinner exchanging unspoken words through their reluctant eyes. David went to watch the highlights of England vs. South Africa, a cricket match on Fox Sports. It was around 9 pm. He didn't know that he had already watched this match LIVE last night. He felt frustrated not understanding why he missed the match. He'd never missed a 'Live' game before.

Sarah cleaned the dishes unmindfully. As the night grew deeper, the sky of her mind became overcast by gray clouds of worries. After watching TV David brushed his teeth two times in one hour before going to bed, knowing he did it only once. They went to bed wordless that night covering themselves in the mild autumnal coolness.

That night Sarah couldn't sleep a wink; slumber land was a forbidden place for her. Oddly enough, she tried to count stars, staring at the ceiling.

Next morning, the first thing David thought he should do was to brush his teeth as he realized that he did forget to brush his teeth last night. After being refreshed, he started to look for their pet Ruth all over the house forgetting she died last week and he was the one who buried her near river Dart. Sarah was still asleep. He prepared porridge for himself and had finished it before she woke up. He fried eggs, mushrooms and made some grilled oatcakes for Sarah as he knew from decades ago how she loved grilled oatcakes with a mug of tea for breakfast. While preparing the meal, he added salt several times, believing he sprinkled it only once.

And when Sarah woke up that morning, she was surprised that David made her breakfast after such a long time. She didn't like oatcakes anymore and she was quite certain that David knew it. It saddened her even more understanding that David must have forgotten that too.

Sarah was completely mystified by the realization that something was wrong with her husband. She began to worry visualizing him as a patient with amnesia.

After spending a frozen night of silence with David, the next morning she decided to make an appointment with Dr. Bruce Miles, their family physician. It was a sunny day full of life just exactly how David liked it to be. He spent most of the morning with some memories of his past, looking vacantly at the typical South West English clouds floating across the blue sky. Then he went to the backyard in search of the lawnmower, not knowing why he wanted it. Suddenly he remembered the day when he first came to live in this house at Devon 25 years ago after selling their old house at Essex. He felt it was just yesterday when Sarah gave birth to their only child, Alice, here in Devon. He failed to recall where Alice lived now. His mind was all buried in the long lost past; trapped in the cobweb of numerous incidents.

He went upstairs and found Sarah was in the bathroom taking shower. He knocked the door asking her, "Did I have my breakfast today? I feel hungry."

"Yes, you did, Dave" Sarah replied in an anxious tone while water ran down her body trying to rinse all her anxieties away. She knew David had already forgotten that today was the doctor's appointment and all the reports would be delivered after the diagnosis.

Sarah went down stairs after shower and found David reading the newspaper from 3 days ago. She exclaimed in frustration, "You've read it seven times so far! Can you remember?"

"This is the first time I'm reading this, sweetheart", replied David. "Don't be so mean to me, please!" he said as if a child so annoyed on his mother for her unjust accusations.

Later that day David was getting ready to go out with Sarah. He went in front of the mirror to comb his hair and surprisingly discovered that his hair had already been combed. In his forgetfulness he wondered who combed his hair…when?…and how? Staring at his own reflection, he was suddenly lost in a queer contemplation. The colour of his shirt reminded him of the navy blue shade from his leather bound diary that he used to write in during his college days. He felt the need of finding that diary again.

That day Sarah took him to Dr. Miles who confirmed David was a patient in the early stages of Alzheimer's disease saying, "Mr. Ashcroft, I know you won't be able to remember this, but I'm sorry to say you are having progressive mental deterioration, which is the most common cause of premature senility."

David couldn't believe this initially, looking straight into the doctor's eyes. He had never been aware of his memory that much because of his confidence in his brain's excellent quality of recollection throughout his life. After a while he looked away, turning a blind eye to the doctor's melancholic face because, during that moment, David wanted to feel nothing but the glorious sun from his school days, constantly shining on his aging mind: a mind that can no more form a new memory.

There was a little teardrop glistening at the corner of Sarah's eye like a pearl, which needed to be hidden because of its preciousness. She tried to conceal her tears by looking down on the diagnosis reports, pretending to read them; and her misty eyes with blurred vision couldn't afford to read a single line.

Dr. Miles kept on explaining the reasons why David had encountered such a disease long before he turned seventy. Sarah's ears seemed to be deafened by an unknown chaos from her overstressed mind. The only cause the doctor explained that she could hear was David's excessive passion for smoking cigarettes.

Dr. Miles stated all the things that David should do from now on. David was perplexed. He kept forgetting why he even had to be in the doctor's chamber.

They left the doctor's office at around 4:15pm. Sarah was driving their 18 year old black Jaguar, which perhaps bore more loving memories than she could ever create. David appeared to be very naive as he kept on asking her the same questions so many times. "Where have we been, Sarah?" ... "Where are you driving to?"

"We went to visit Dr. Bruce Miles, sweetheart!" Sarah replied for the third time.

Sarah's eternal love for David was stronger than her patience. And her love became remarkably forbearing in time, which made her respond to his repeatedly asking questions many times.

She never failed him. She believed- I never will.

Right now life seemed utterly obstructive to her. At the moment she wanted to concentrate only on driving, forgetting the world. The sun was going to sink very soon while David's favourite twilight began to appear. Sarah noticed some beautiful birds going back to their nests flying towards the crimson west; just like she and David were returning to their home. That made her smile.

Suddenly she heard her beloved asking, "Where have we been, Sarah?"

"We went to visit Dr. Bruce Miles, sweetheart!" she replied with all her loving heart.

Another World

Aafia was staring at the black, fumed sky imagining it pouring down cauldron of repressed anger. She no more wanted to hear the maelstrom of weapons clanging. Yet she had no choice but to lay down on the sodden ground yielding to the bloody ichor. Her muteness had nothing to explain, since she had lost her six year old son two hours ago before she realized that she lost her left leg too. Her agonizing heart was numb, empty enough to want to cease to exist.
She didn't know where her husband went because he had been missing, ever since the fighting broke out in Homs, Syria's third largest city. No matter how large the city was Aafia's world became the smallest planet in a mordant universe of war.

The trauma within her was pounding as if it was her head having a nervous system of its own, losing some sanity after the severe air strike. Life kept her alive but her little son was dead in front of her whose soulless body had already been taken away.

Her husband, Omar befriended some of those men who seized the Syrian government's largest military base in Deraa. The last time she had lunch with Omar was over a month ago and she couldn't recall any dinner with him for a long time.

Suddenly a scream of a young child undeafened her and she began to hear wailing all around. She saw spritz of blood sluiced the broken legs of an old bench just four feet away from her. Just then she remembered what happened… She went out for hanging her washed-wet clothes on a rack under the sun this morning, when the ransacking of bombs or bullets (she could not tell) started to devastate the area. Ayman, her little son, was helping his mother drying the clothes, not knowing his life would reach its complete dryness attaining mortality in just few hours time.

All of a sudden Aafia began to feel hallucinated, sensing hot wind whipped at her scarred face to wound her some more. Her pounding head stopped spinning, but then it was her longing for death which began to spin all around her. She did not wish to live anymore. During this state of comatose, she heard some swishes and hisses replacing the thundery noise of painful scream which surrounded her, as though Omar was hissing (like a venomous serpent) instead of whispering and the only thing she could hear him repeatedly uttering- Deraa city in March 2011… Deraa city in March 2011… Deraa city in March 2011. Her leg began to bleed until she took her last breath. And only God knew why she had to leave; perhaps to accompany her very young son…

Author's Note: 'Deraa City in March 2011' is the place and date when the Syrian conflict started

Elinóra's Judgment

Long time ago there lived a queen in Iceland. Her name was Elinóra, but people used to call her Coldy, because her whole body was uniquely made with icy cool flesh as if God's miraculous creation to represent a Nordic Island.
Unlike her outward form, her heart was so full of warmth. And when she sat on her throne, she looked as pure and celestial as a white swan reigning on a tranquil lake in a frosty winter. Everybody loved her; not only because of her indomitable beauty, but also because of her generosity and tenderness. And so did two friends: Aaron and Alfar.

Both of them were 21-year-old inhabitants of a village called Þórshöfn which was nearby the castle where Queen Elinóra lived in the northeast region of Iceland. Aaron was a very attractive, tall, young man, while Alfar was a dwarf with only four feet two inches of height. Aaron was being called Flamingo by Alfar, as whenever they were out and about together, Alfar felt like a Puffin having a hard time to cope with Aaron's longer strides. Nevertheless, Alfar was very proud of his bosom friend Aaron's good look.

Like most of the young men in the village, both of them had an unrequited longing to meet Coldy, the beautiful queen who was nothing but an unfathomable dream to them.

"I want to kiss her hand bowing to her on a moon-blessed night", Aaron said to Alfar dreaming through his fantasy on the unreachable queen.

"And I want to kiss her feet praising her heavenly beauty on a refreshing spring afternoon", Alfar replied in an intoxicated manner as though he was doing it right then.

Village people were forbidden to go to the castle and that was the rule everyone had to abide by. Yet one day Aaron and Alfar seriously decided to venture to visit the queen. They knew that the queen was extremely kind, therefore, they realized that if they could reach the castle somehow, the queen might forgive their disobedience.

One sunlit afternoon both the friends started their expedition towards the castle in hope to meet the queen for once. It was near evening when they finally arrived near the gate of the castle. That was for the first time they had seen any castle in the entire life. Aaron could not take his eyes off the white, stony grandeur of the queen's home. And Alfar was left totally wordless by the ancient beauty the castle walls reflected upon his awestruck mind. From a distance, they saw two huge well built guards right next to the castle gate. They planned to lie in wait into a bush nearby until someone arrived at the castle gate. All they needed was the gate to be opened so that they could secretly enter.

Suddenly, Aaron began to feel jealous of Alfar thinking he should not take Alfar inside. He wanted to be the only one to be able to meet the cold beauty. He desired to see her alone to hold her hand. His jealous mind evoked many negative thoughts against Alfar and he didn't want him to be with him at all. But he had not expressed it to Alfar yet.

All of a sudden a big horse-drawn wagon came closer to the Castle which instantly led the guards to open the gate.

"Hurry up! Get a move on, mate!" Alfar whispered to Aaron as he quietly jumped out of the bushes running towards the gate. He, being very short in size, managed to hide himself from the keen eye sights of the castle guards. He safely reached the lawn of the castle. But unfortunately Aaron stepped out of the bush, all so reckless with his suppressed excitement totally exposed. So, he miserably failed to remain hidden from the guards.

The guards found a tall village man, with poverty inscribed on all over his appearance, trying to trespass into the castle on the sly. The guards caught him immediately. One of them yelled at Aaron saying – "Who the hell are you?! How dare you want to be inside the castle!"

"My name is Aaron. I am here to meet the beautiful queen: Coldy. Please, allow me to see her."- Aaron begged, being on his knees, looking straight into the guard's eyes. His envious mind couldn't bear the anguish that Alfar managed to get inside the castle when he, himself, failed. So, to the guard he further said, "There is a tiny man who already has slipped into the gate. Why can't you arrest him too?"

In no time, the guards ran inside the castle lawn, ransacking every corner of the place and discovered Alfar hiding himself underneath a massive oak tree a few yards away from the gate. They arrested him too. Alfar was quivering in fearful agitation and only terror seemed to be radiating from his face.

"I am A…Al…Alfar. I…I…I…want to meet the queen. Yes, I'm here to…to…to… meet her. Noting else. Only to meet her." - Alfar cried out loud as he was nervously stuttering. "My friend Aaron is here to see her as well. Please forgive us and let us meet her, Please!" Alfar exclaimed.

Immediately they were taken to the prison. And the prison-warden informed the queen about the whole incident seeking for her command about what they should do with these two newly imprisoned men.

The queen was renowned for her kindness. She felt curious about them. She said, "Okay. I'll decide later. Let me talk to them first"

"I need to know what they want. Bring them one by one to me." the queen said and ordered.

At first it was Alfar's turn. He was taken to the queen as Aaron was left alone into the prison cell. Envy inside of Aaron reached its peak. He was literally shaking in an envious wrath as he felt that he was loathing Alfar more than ever now.

Now, Alfar was standing in front of the queen with his little body bowed down. The tremble of his small knees reminded him of how insignificant he was.

"So, what brought you here?" Queen Goldy asked scrutinizing him from his head to toe.

"Me and my friend, we, just wanted to meet you for once, only once in a life time, Your Majesty!", he replied with a lower voice in all humbleness.

"My friend, Aaron. He is a great guy. We both decided to come to see you for once. Please forgive us. We have no other intention. Please forgive us. Our purpose is served. We've met and have seen you now. So, please forgive and permit us to go"

"Okay. I understand, the queen said. "Do you want to see me again in future?"- she further asked curiously.

"O! Your Majesty! That will be under your mercy. Only your kind wish could bring the two of us back to this castle again" Alfar replied with his drowned heart lifted up a bit.

"All right. You can go now", said the queen.

Then Aaron was brought before the Queen up next. He took a bow before her, feeling that he was the most fortunate man in the world, the king of the world. He could only see the white cold skin of the queen; but alas! he could never touch it.

"Now tell me why did you dare to come to the castle?"- the queen asked staring at the very good looking village man, Aaron.

"I am here only to see you as I heard of your breath taking beauty, Your Majesty. And I just wanted to see you. Nothing else.", replied Aaron. Then with an envious mind he further proclaimed – "There is a dwarf with me named: Alfar who you met few minutes ago, you can ignore him. He must be having a vague dream to become a king. You can keep him in prison, if you want. But please forgive me and my innocence and allow me to go" "Okay. I understand, said the queen. "Do you want to see me again in future?"- she further asked.

"Oh, I'd love to see you again, Your Majesty." I want to come to visit you, to see you always. Don't worry I'll never bring any tiny man again. Rest assured."

"All right. You can go now", said the queen.

Both Aaron and Alfar were taken back to the prison until the queen gave her verdict.

Queen Elinóra had a heart full of kindness and mercy. From her heart she didn't want to punish poor village people who only came to see her. But she sensed Aaron's envy towards his own friend Alfar. Her heart of mercy couldn't forgive that. Whereas, Alfar was purely honest remaining loyal and kind to his friend Aaron. So, the insightful Queen made her decision. The next morning the verdict given by Queen Elinóra was declared in public-

Aaron was ordered to be taken out of the castle under the condition that he could never come near the area of the castle ever again. If he would ever attempt to come, he would be sentenced to lifelong incarceration. Alfar was also ordered to be freed from the prison but at the same time merciful queen Elinóra granted his wish to visit the castle whenever he wanted.

Moral Of the Story: Envy has no place in a heart of mercy

Author's note:

I have tried to create a fairy tale fiction here with a moral of the story in the end. Being a classic story lover, I am inspired to write a story which would have a moral in conclusion…kind of like Aesop's fables.

Vacation of Innocence

It was 12th July, 1970. The sun in Kraków was warmer than last week when for the first time in life James came to visit Poland. James H Robinson, a 50-year-old geotechnical engineer from Southern California needed some isolation after being very tired working with the committee who developed grading and excavation codes in the Los Angeles area.

He left his job two months ago declaring himself retired because his current life wanted to see him in a former status for a different kind of future. He accepted the reality when his personal physician so indifferently revealed that the reason of his shortness of breath was Alpha-1 antitrypsin deficiency. His curious mind then got to know that it was a genetic disorder which was first described just a few years ago.

But the doctor comforted him not to worry. So, his long time dream of 'visiting Germany and Poland someday' eventually brought him to enjoy a twenty five days summer vacation here in Europe. And his love for medieval architecture and Jewish heritage inspired him to stay more in Poland rather than in any western European country.

He could not believe that it had already been three days since he left Warsaw. He still felt thrilled because of the amazing time he spent in the city, the name of which no one can pronounce, Łódź. He just wished he could leave his finger prints on one of those 19th-century machinery and fabrics displayed in the Central Museum of Textiles there in Łódź.

He arrived here in Kraków this morning thanking the Polish railway service in his mind for the exemplary punctuality. He planned to go for a walk to revel in the neoclassical look of those old brick buildings in the colourful Main Square where the illustrious culture was deeply rooted.

By the time James reached the main market square it was nearly midday. Summer invited the tree leaves to be greener than ever before as though branches were delighted welcoming the good looking appearance of an American here in the old town district of Kraków. James looked at the clear blue sky which, he felt, was bestowing some gratitude towards him for coming to visit.

He started walking into the center of the square, dominated by the renaissance style Cloth Hall. His eyes were glued on the stalls displaying variety of exclusive imports from the east. He decided not to purchase anything from any of the shops here; window shopping might suit his lonesome trip this time he thought. He preferred to take pictures and kept on capturing the moments as soon as he reached the Gothic towers of St. Mary's Basilica. At first he went to take some photographs of the exquisiteness of the church from the Mikołajska Street which had quite a different view. Then again he came back to the front to take more pictures of this 262 ft tall elegant architecture. His passion for photography engulfed him. He wished someone could help him to capture his own image in front of this finest 14th century masterpiece.

He was looking around if he could ask someone to take his picture with the assistance of his long time friend of a camera: Yashica Atoron. Suddenly he saw a very beautiful lady with an angelic face wearing a soft baby blue chiffon dress (long enough to reach her knees) was walking past him. There was something amazing in her style of walking which beguiled his mind for a while and he didn't quite sure why he loved that matching fabric belt (which had tiny white polka dot on it) so delicately wrapped around her perfect waist.

Even though he was unsure if she could understand English, he had to stop her saying – "Excuse me Ma'am". And she stopped being confused, if it was actually her he meant to talk to. She looked back and stared directly at him and the brightness of her green eyes twinkled upon his grey eyes which seemed so curious having flecks of gold and brown.

"Yes", she answered in a modest manner with such naivety that only a lovely woman from the Eastern Europe can have, he thought.

"If you don't mind, can you please take a picture of me in front of this church tower?"- James hesitatingly asked with a lowered voice as he clearly felt his raising heartbeats.

"Sure I can. Show me how to use your camera", answered the stranger lady who James believed was one of the beautiful ladies in the world. And her English with very natural Polish accent, to him, seemed like the most amazing and flawless sound his ears could ever wish to hear.

"Thank you very much. Here it is. It has fully automatic shutter with exposure up to 8 seconds. You just press this button", handing over his camera to her he said.

"Sure, Okay. You stand right there at the middle", she smiled and replied pointing her right hand's forefinger to the center of the brick gothic church.

James walked backwards and then tried to pose standing straight, putting a gentle smile on his face with his hand folded on his chest. He felt nervous and a bit uneasy.

She held the camera up and through the lens she secretly gazed upon his beautiful eyes. And as if she could feel his nervousness she said – "Ready? Don't be shy. Smile a bit more. There you go!"- As she finished clicking, she returned the camera to James. And James with a broad smile on his almost dried up lips said- "Thank you!" Then he extended his right hand towards her saying "I'm James Robinson. Nice to meet you"

While shaking his hand, she felt the coldness of his palm through her warm skin. "I'm Zuzanna Wisniewski. Very nice to meet you too Mr. Robinson.", she said.

Deep down inside James didn't want to say good bye to her so, he further added- "Beautiful name. Are you from Kraków?"

"Dziękuję Ci. Yes, I live near St. Florian's Gate, and you?", Zuzanna replied even though she had already guessed that this stranger man could be a tourist all the way from the US because of his very American accent. She loved his manly appearance of six feet 2 inches of height and her emotional heart wished he could ask her for a walk. Both of them started walking side by side, not knowing where the path would lead them to.

"I'm a retired engineer from California. I just came to visit Poland last week." James replied very anxiously looking at her curly blond hair with much adoration glittering from his loving eyes. And in his unconscious mind he thought he should have met this amazing lady 15 years ago when his wife left him and he never got married again.

With a nervous voice hesitatingly he asked- "Can we go for a walk? I mean, if you have time…"

"Aren't we walking already?" Zuzanna answered with a mystical smile on her lips as usual. And her retort made James laugh a lot and to hide the laughter he put his head down. Then he noticed her footsteps bearing her amazing velvet white shoes are no less attractive than a beautiful future he could dream of…with her…

"So, is this your home town?", he asked while listening to the hypnotic trumpet signal called the Hejnał mariacki which was being played from the top of the taller of Saint Mary's two towers

"No, I'm originally from Łódź but I'm a school teacher around here near Kraków Barbican"- Zuzanna replied comfortably wanting this afternoon walk with this stranger man never to end. Being a single mother of one child, her life seemed to have lost its spark holding on to the dutiful fire burning in the hearth of life.

Together they were walking towards the main entrance of the church. Both of them wanted to go inside together but owing to their inexpressible ego they didn't quite understand how to express the willingness to each other. Finally James gathered a little courage and said- "I've heard of the precious Veit Stoss Altar Piece, would you like to visit?"

"I wish I could, but I have to go now because my friend is moving to Russia and I need to see her off. Besides, the altar piece remains closed most of the time for public, even on Sundays in order to preserve its mystery within" – replied Zuzanna wishing she could stay but she really had to leave, she knew, because her friend Zofia who's living for Moscow tonight, would meet her at 3:00 pm and in fact, she came here to buy some gifts for Zofia.

"Oh, forgive me, I didn't realize that. It was so wonderful to meet you. I'd love to see you once more. Can we meet again?" -said James swallowing his ego expecting with all his heart that Zuzanna would say 'Yes'.

"Yes, sure. Why not? I'd love that" Zuzanna answered not knowing why she wanted to meet him again when she hardly know him. She thought- sometimes a heart has its own reason that a mind could not tell.

"Alright then I'll be right there in front of the Adam Mickiewicz Monument tomorrow at 12 noon and we could go to lunch together somewhere, okay?" said James staring at her graceful face as he couldn't take his eyes off her. Zuzanna looked younger than her age. Even though she celebrated her 40th birthday last month, James thought she could be around thirty two. James loved the way how her lovely voice trembled by her shyness when she said, "Yes, sure. I'll see you tomorrow at 12. Bye bye then"

As she left, James felt that a strange feeling surrounded him while he saw her walking down the street of the main market square. He looked up at the towers of the basilica which highlighted the sky line of the city and wanted to go back to his hotel only to fall into a deep slumber so that tomorrow could come fast.

Zuzanna went to bed early that night bidding adieu to her friend Zofia. She couldn't stop thinking about the last afternoon and she was confused why she wanted to meet him again. She could feel that she liked that brown haired American man a lot and there was a wild flicker of light into his eyes where she really wanted to get lost.

The next morning at 7:10am James woke up with his terrible illness of breathlessness, realizing his inherited genetic disorder came back with its recurring respiratory infection, fatigue, and rapid heartbeat which just had began to haunt him again. His head was spinning because he was struggling to take breath. He just remembered he forgot to take medicine last night, since he couldn't get Zuzanna out of his forgetful mind.

He called the hotel emergency and asked them to immediately take him to the hospital. His world fell apart because he knew right then that he would not be able to go to meet her at the

Adam Mickiewicz Monument this afternoon. He tried to breathe and breathe harder recollecting the memory of Zuzanna's heavenly existence which spellbound him. James was taken to the "Szpital Uniwersytecki w Krakowie" at around 8 O'clock while he was in completely unconscious state. The doctors understood that he had a stroke because of the blood's flow to the brain being blocked and he needed to be treated in here in the hospital for an uncertain period of time.

Zuzanna reached near the remarkable bronze monument at around 11:50pm, wearing her favorite red dress as if she wanted to be a 'lady in red' for James. She knew that it was nothing like 'love at first sight' but perhaps something more than that. She kept on eagerly waiting (pretending to be one of those tourists who came to see the beauty of this 18th century masterpiece) and she loved this time span of waiting for someone who, she believed, achieved a special place in her heart. She could not wait to know him more.

She began walking around the magnificent statue of Adam Mickiewicz (the greatest Polish Romantic poet), since it had already been forty five minutes she was there standing but James had not appeared yet. After an hour and thirty minutes of waiting, Zuzanna felt utterly frustrated, sad and insulted. Several questions started to ruin her mind - was it just a game from a stranger man? Or did he totally forget about today's meeting? Was everything okay with him?

She looked around in search of that wonderfully gentle face she liked so much, but all she could find was nothing but hopelessness from the features of many unknown strangers and passersby. She began to regret how she could even forget to ask James which hotel he was in when she didn't have any contact information of him.

After two hours of waiting she was standing at the south side of Adam Mickiewicz Monument- right in front of the part called 'Muse of Poetry With Child' and while gazing at the amazing woman and the little girl made of bronze, she imagined it was her daughter and herself when life became as frozen and lifeless as it was for this sculptural glory. Then she decided to leave not knowing why she even cared to come. Her misty eyes failed to hold back tears and her wrist watch showed 3pm when she returned home.

Meet Me at Sunset in Vlora

I could never forget how wonderfully she uttered her name, Vlora "Please don't ask me many questions. My head is pounding and I already can tell that the Italian night must be darker and longer than any other night in the world."- said Vlora, one of the injured refugees from Albania who, I as a team leader of a temporary liaison team from the UNHCR, had to interview. She kept on describing the morbid pictures imprinted on her perturbed memory from the past few days. She didn't know what to do with her aching arms when she recalled her body was hanging from a ladder in a cargo ship for a very long time. Being a passenger in a voyage of 36 hours with no food, no drinking water Vlora had little strength to allow her mind to be completely functional. But apparently she didn't forget the name of the ship as oddly enough she and that horrid cargo monster shared the same name.

The irony of fate was- this beautiful Albanian lady whose birthday was on 7th August, boarded the ship named Vlora (which was built in 1960 in Ancona, Italy) on 7th August 1991 and I was born on August 7 in the year 1960. And I still didn't know why I felt very connected to her. Perhaps, 7th August had something to do with that. But to me, 8th August, 1991 bore more significance because I met her on that very day.

I wondered how a woman could still be looking so attractive after all the vulnerability. She appeared to be in her early 20s and her dark brown hair was shiny enough to suppress the darkness of her surroundings. I was observing every blink of her amazing gray eyes that offered light of hope. Even though her neurotic numbness seized her, it initially hid the pain of the 2nd degree burns to her neck, face and shoulders. She loathed the horrid temperature which reached the high 90s.

"I wish the ship could be docked at the port of Brindisi around 4am, like it was previously planned, so that I could have saved myself from 7 hours of additional torment, squeezing body to body with thousands of wretched people."- Vlora further said as I was asking her how the journey went on altogether from the coastal city of Durrës to Bari.

"I never wanted to be in Italy. I didn't want to be a part of this unprecedented mass", said Vlora and her weak, trembling lips showed no sign of inner fragility.

"My mother died last year in a car accident and my father fled to the south in Greece with his new girl friend. He asked me to move out with them as I was alone. But I didn't want to", Vlora kept on saying, even though I didn't ask her about all those personal details.

"I've been jobless for quite a while and the idea of rapid privatization of the agricultural sector seemed never to work for me because I used to work in a bank which collapsed", she further said.

"Actually, we were hoping the restructuring of the economy in your country earlier last year would help, but unfortunately it rather brought more crisis", I said.

"Yes, and the turmoil for the fall of communism indeed paved the way to this economic collapse. One of my neighbours suggested me to enter the compound of the German embassy. But I never listened. Now I regret. What will be my fate here in Italy? I'm hopelessly helpless now", Vlora said without pausing; as if she had to tell me everything in one breath. And I sensed a wave of fearful insecurity coming from the sound of her wonderful voice. Her English accent was very good. I wondered how. Her physical agony seemed to be avoided by her metal anxiety and torment as she was still spontaneous in describing her misfortune.

Vlora was the only woman amongst the seven refugees that I had to interview that day. I knew that I needed to put an end to my conversation with her real soon; but strangely enough I didn't want to lose her. I didn't want her to be out of trace. So, I was hurried to introduce myself to her.

"My name is Giovanni Moretti. I'm currently working as a director of an aiding team from the UNHCR", I said. Then I gave her my business card. And I strongly remember that instead of giving her Italian lira, I gave her forty Euros in coins and some treasury notes. And I could clearly recall that she couldn't believe those coins and notes and she was asking – "Are you from the US?"

"Sorry, I am not familiar with this kind of notes and coins. These notes look like they're from the US government", she added. And I saw mistrustful curiosity into her confused eyes. So, I comforted her as much as I could.

"No, I'm not from the US. But I told you that am working at the UNHCR. I'll help you to settle here in Italy. Rest assured." I said.

"How can I trust you? I don't know you at all; besides, you've given me some strange currency that I have never seen before. How do you think I may trust you?", asked Vlora.

"Don't worry at all. I will give you a cell phone tomorrow. I shall meet you here again tomorrow, okay?" I said.

"Cell phone? Do you mean Nokia C-MicroPlus kind of thing? But it's kind of expensive. You can bring me Nokia 10 which was out in January, if you want…ha ha ha", Said Vlora making me very surprised as she started to laugh. (How come a person laughing like that in such a hazardous condition- I had no clue)

"No, I'm not joking. I will bring you iphone. And I know you have never heard of it either" I replied.

She stared at me…completely wordless. And I knew that even her steady, insistent gaze would not be able to fathom what I was talking about. It was nearing midday when I had to say Goodbye to Vlora assuring her that I'd meet her tomorrow here in the hospital near this Adriatic port where she was being taken earlier this morning.

Being the team leader of the emergency aid, I had to leave because of my other essential errands on that very Thursday. But I couldn't wait to see Vlora again on the next day.

Sadly, orders straight from Rome arrived which commanded the authority to keep all the Albanian refugees in the port of Bari and to send them back to Albania. I came to know from my boss that after an emergency meeting of Prime Minister Giulio Andreotti's Cabinet in Rome the orders were actually issued on late Wednesday.

Deep down inside I thanked my boss at UNHCR for waking me up this morning with his urgent phone call saying- "Giovanni, a radarless ship has just arrived in early morning today with excessive weight of passenger presence. The captain said that due to suffocating heat and lack of water, they have thousands of injured people abroad who are so dehydrated that they even cut the ship's cooling tube open to cool themselves. We need to take care of them"

When I arrived at the Bari port, it was very hurtful to witness all those disillusioned Albanians whose wish for a better life turned into a dreamless misery now.

The next morning at around 5:30am I woke up and as promised I took my iPhone 4 (that I purchased in April, 2011but never used) for Vlora.

I knew that this was insane and no one would believe the truth that I was leading my life in a parallel condition of realities between two time frames. I knew researchers would label it as "Mandela Effect" or may be 'False Memory' kind of thing. But this was what I had been going through. I hoped only Vlora could understand me and would believe me…but then I wondered why would she…

The clear sky of Bari was extraordinarily blue that Friday morning when I reached the hospital gate as if it wanted to pour down some pure blessings so that my uncanny life could make some sense.

The young doctor from the emergency who took care of Vlora yesterday was Lorenzo Bianchi. When I enquired about her, Dr. Bianchi said – "At first she was about to be taken to the La Vittoria Sports Stadium, but then we realized she was too sick to endure that; so we decided to send her to board one of those five air force planes to Albania."

But before she left, she wanted me to give you this note Mr. Moretti. The doctor handed me over a pale piece of paper where she wrote "Meet me at sunset in Vlora…you know how. Only a year more and we'll have our years".

"Ok, grazie, dottore."- I said. "Dr. Bianchi, Can you tell me her full name?" I asked.

"No, I don't know, I'm afraid. She was enlisted only with her first name.", said the doctor.

By the time I got out of the hospital it was around 10:30 in the morning. Even the powerful sun seemed lifelessly weak to me. I had no idea how to meet her in Vlora as I had no way of finding her in Albania without a surname. So many unprecedented thoughts came to my restive mind. What if I could meet her in the parallel world from the future that I have been dealing with.

Time was passing faster than my restless heartbeats and I had to relate to things to connect with Vlora. I knew I would meet her in Sunset somehow…but in Vlora…?…how? Did she indicate something secretive in her note? Then I began to wonder.

The next year, 1992 was very crucial for me as I knew that would be the time to eventually link with Vlora. I didn't know which year or how I could be able to find her, but I had a strong feeling through the hint of her visceral note that similar events in our lives in the year 1992 would connect us to the parallel world where we would be able to meet.

I knew she was in Albania and I felt a strong telepathic connection with her not knowing exactly what went on between the weary souls of us. A distance of 233 Kilometers seemed closer than just a mile away.

After the parliamentary election at the end of March 1992 in Albania, the government was weakened by more corruption and poverty. I predicted that the Democratic Party of Albania's winning of the nation's first free election would lead the country to a civil war sooner or later. I strongly felt that was the time when Vlora would connect to another time frame; because her life surely had become miserably purposeless at her own country then.

At the same time my life became miserable after the general election in Italy in April 1992. I did quit my job at UNHCR and I just wanted to escape from the Annus horribilis. 1992 was like the end of an era for the Italian politics but to me this year was like a road to a new beginning of my life. The bomb that killed Giovanni (not me of course; I meant Falcone) on May 23 blew me away in utter despair and the massive killings in the summer '92 made me want to cease to live. I wanted to get rid of the time of the Sicilian mafia. Only my hope to meet Vlora at sunset in Vlora, Albania kept me alive. And I felt that I began to disappear from this realm of cruel Italian time and was setting out towards the year 2011 again.

The next morning it was 8th August, 2011, the 20th anniversary of the Arrival at Bari for the Italians and for the Albanians. The municipality of Bari started celebrating the memory with a week of events of arts and cultures. I was going to join the other Memorial events but I didn't because I decided to catch the flight to Vlora, Albania later that day.

But I attended one event in the morning at Bari where people gathered in solidarity. I could never forget what Mayor Michele Emiliano said on the presentation of the memorial event. He said- "It is clear that the 'Missione Vlora' is not exhausted even if 20 years have passed…because today we have the possibility to put together many emotions that make Bari, since then, a multicultural city. Twenty years ago the secret of our city was just that…Open the doors to the difference"

I could relate to the Mayor's words. I knew that my own 'Mission Vlora' could never be exhausted either. And the weight of anticipation I carried in my heart was heavier than the 8600-ton Vlora itself.

Suddenly I wanted to visit the hospital near the city's 60-year-*old, empty,* Della Vittoria soccer stadium where I met Vlora. It had been 20 years; but I knew it was only a year for me. I got into the hospital and while walking through the lobby I realized I needed to meet Dr. Bianchi.

"Is Dr. Lorenzo Bianchi still working here?"- I asked the lady at the reception.

"No, but his daughter Sofia Bianchi works as a nurse here now- how can I help you, Sir?", said the receptionist.

"Will you please tell his daughter that Giovanni Moretti, a former officer from The UN Refugee Agency, wants to talk to her? And it's urgent.", I said.

After a telephonic conversation with Sofia Bianchi, the receptionist allowed me to get into the hallway saying- please go to room number 7 at end of this wing.

And as soon as I got in, I found a beautiful young lady sitting in the room. She looked so like Vlora having the same silky, beautiful, black hair and the exact dazzling blink of eyes. I was stuck for words for a while.

"Hello, Mr. Moretti. Nice to meet you. I'm Vlora Besjana's daughter. My mom told me everything about you." said Sofia with a gentle smile in her face and I couldn't believe my eyes that she had her mother's smile. It took me a second to realize what a loser I was.

"Hi, Good to meet you Sofia. I'm so sorry I failed your mother. But trust me I was about to go to Vlora, Albania tonight, even though I didn't know how to find your mom there", I said.

"My mother used to go to the ship Vlora almost every sunset because the ship stayed in the Bari's port for 45 days more", said Sofia.

"Do you remember her note? She asked you to meet her in Vlora at Sunset; but you never came. My mom was very stupidly impulsive and she thought after a year you and her could be together", Sofia added.

"Oh, my God, I thought she meant the City of Vlora, in Albania. I completely misunderstood her note"- my heart was aching as I replied to Sofia.

"My mom never boarded the plane because she believed you would come and so, she wanted to wait near the ship for you at sunset. Unfortunately, you never arrived there. She came back to the hospital to my father for a regular treatment on her burnt ailment and they got married in 7th August 1992 and I am the result of their successful matrimonial life as you can see…ha ha ha" Sofia began to laugh exactly like her mother.

"Where is your mom and dad now?", I asked.

"They permanently live in *Sicily*- our home town, as they recently moved out there." said Sofia.

Suddenly I knew that I was so right to get away from the Sicilian people.

"You know the eerie thing, Mr. Moretti? Me and my dad always believe that you met mom once more just a few years back because of some Euro coins which my mother always keeps with her saying you gave her those coins in 1991 when there was no Euro coin at all."- Sofia further said.

Right then I hated myself so much for experiencing events from a different reality, from different time frames. No one would believe me I knew, rather people would accuse me of having false memories…but I believed Vlora would understand that I never lied. People told me that I might be creating false memories, but the truth was - my entity was being haunted by false hope all these years.

I hated to know what time it was when I left the hospital because 'time' appeared to be the real disaster of my life. I left the hospital with a broken heart as unmendable as it could be, asking myself – what's the purpose of loving and living? What's the reason of keeping our memories alive?

Author's Note: This story I've written imagining that it is an excerpt from the diary of my protagonist Giovanni Moretti, an officer of UNHCR. He did interview and fell in love with Vlora Besjana, an injured Albanian refugee from the ship of Vlora in 1991.

Later Giovanni Moretti was suffering from the psychological phenomenon called "False Memory". In reality, after 1991 both of them accidentally met again in *Sicily, in 2005 when* Giovanni actually gave her the Euro coins and treasury notes. But due to his mental state of illness he thought he was leading a parallel life while describing his memory of Vlora Besjana. The sadness of losing Vlora made him this way. He never stopped waiting to meet Vlora Besjana at sunset in Vlora. Everything he wrote in his diary was true except for only the time shifting fantasy of memory he created. The year 1991 remained with him endlessly and he felt that he was living a parallel life. All characters here are indeed imaginary.

Never Far Away

Everything had changed in Amanda's life since 2008. Amanda Merchant, a young nurse from Froedtert Hospital, *Milwaukee* had been under mental treatment for many years. Ever since she left the Vigil service in 2008 at World Youth Day in Sydney, a new chapter had begun in the book of her life.

Amanda was in love with an Australian school teacher, Liam Johnson who took her to Brisbane at his father's home for a 25-day-vacation in summer 2008. And from there, with her Liam drove 914km away to attend the 23rd World Youth Day in Sydney. Amanda was always a God loving person and Liam loved her so much for her everlasting faith in God as in modern days most people seemed to have no trust in the almighty Lord.

Amanda and Liam suddenly planned to visit Sydney. He booked a cheap 2 star hotel to save some money as he desired to travel other parts of Australia with his beloved. As they knew from 15th July the youth festival would continue until 20th, they decided to stay in Sydney until the early morning of the 21st. But fate planned something different for them, something blood-curdling and unearthly.

At first Liam wanted to console himself by believing it was something extraterrestrial which should have a scientific explanation, but as time went by it came out as a fatal demonic experience Liam ever had in his entire 26 years life.

It was from the 19th July Amanda refused to eat food. The traditional Australian menu they were being served in the festival: she stopped eating altogether. The smell of the meat pies, slices of bread and the serving of Weet-Bix Crunch made her puke two times that day.

"Let's get back to the hotel, Liam", said Amanda and while started walking she wished Liam could guide her unflinching steps.

The crowd from the festival seemed to have disappeared faster from Amanda's hazy sight than the lingering voice inside of her head constantly telling her- 'Run, Amanda! Run away from here!!'

Liam decided to get back allowing her to rest in the quietness at the hotel. It was about 4:30pm when they returned. The sun was not scorching enough upon the trees to highlight the limbs of the silky oaks. The weather was comforting, however, at the hotel lobby Amanda almost fainted as she felt something else was leading her entity. On that very night, the pale skin of Amanda turned into dead white and her green already-sunken-eyes began to have blurred vision as though she drank herself into a rare oblivion.

At around 3am she woke up in the hotel bed and started screaming and cursing – "I hate them. I hate those bastards. I hate them"

"I loathe those bastards who say- "*You will receive power when the Holy Spirit comes upon you*", she kept on saying…

Liam tried his best to calm her down not knowing what happened. He was shocked as the line she uttered was the theme of the festival. She appeared like a demonic witch as she went on cursing at Liam and began to bite him. His right arm instantly started to bleed as Amanda's craziness reached its peak by pushing her long nails through the skin of Liam. Amanda's slender body started shaking as she yelled at Liam – "Take me to the ten horn beast. Why the hell you had to bring me here in Australia. I need to go to the lion, bear and to the leopard."

"Take me to the lion having those eagle's wings, Take me, take me, take me to the bear…and to the leopard too"- Amanda's scream went louder than before as she repeatedly said those words.

"You will all be f**ked with those 7 heads and 10 horns" – she added and her scary face grinned with her tongue out like a serpent swallower monster.

"Amanda, please rest your heart, sweetheart", said Liam as he tried to stay calm, hugging her tight against his chest.

"Take me to England, Russia and Germany. I don't wanna be here"- Amanda wailing at Liam punching his stomach and chest as another manly voice had taken possession of her voice speaking through her throat.

For more than an hour this havoc continued and Liam had been helpless until he realized that an evil spirit possessed to smite Amanda. This horrific entity supplanted her entire consciousness with its own. Amanda, had been pressed down on the bed with an unknown force which tried to throttle her and the outburst of profanity disgusted Liam. He decided to read the bible verses to pacify her. But suddenly he realized that he forgot the holy book at his home. Then he wanted to use the internet of his phone and unfortunately he found it was being disconnected. Now he feared more not knowing how to evict this wicked demon from inside of her. Liam wished he could know about the Saint Michael's Prayer against Satan and the Rebellious Angels, attributed to Pope Leo X. His mind was not working and he could not even remember what his grandpa told him about Section 11 of the Rituale Romanum.

Suddenly the light bulb of the table lamp next to Liam burned out. Yet Amanda was completely able to see in the darkness. Liam knew that Amanda's arms needed to be bound to the bed frame, but it was impossible, since she was getting stronger by the minute than all the strength Liam could gather for himself. Darkness overpowered Amanda and she was continuously spitting on him. She was biting him so hard as if she wanted to eat his flesh. There was a constant gnawing sound coming out of Amanda's mouth as she loudly lashed out at him – "I will dismember you, darling. I have to eat your flesh, Liam, Liam, Liam my love!"

Amanda started uttering most words three times like an evil possessed person with a cynical gaze at Liam. However, her satanic restlessness discontinued as the dawn broke. Her senseless body fell on the bed- fragile and tormented. And Liam thanked the Lord as he believed his prayers had been answered. As the morning sun brought a brief relief to Liam's mind, he decided to contact his dad's friend: Father Joseph.

At around 7O'clock Liam called him at St Mary's Cathedral in Sydney. He explained everything to Father Joseph. Father said she needed to be exorcized soon enough. The demon inside of her indicated things regarding the end time. Specially, this nefarious entity seemed to be an evil worshipper of the beasts mentioned in Daniel

Chapter Seven. Father Joseph said, "This demon might tell more about the fourth beast mentioned in Daniel – 7:23."

"And some more blasphemous things which would cause harm to humanity"- added the father.

"But Lord Jesus will save us"- he whispered.

Then he uttered those holy lines from Matthew 28:6- *"He is not here: for he is risen, as he said. Come, see the place where the Lord lay"*

Suddenly, to his own disappointment, Father Joseph remembered that according to The Sorbonne in 1620 the testimony of demons could not be accepted because demons always lie, even during the time of exorcism. The demon would not reveal any serious information. So, eventually, Father Joseph resolved not to perform the exorcism for Amanda by himself.

The next day Amanda's exorcism was performed by Father Gregory, a clairvoyant exorcist who dared to take the entity in his own body and then expelled it. The possessing spirit was so bad and it fled very late at the sign of the cross and holy water. Amanda's mind was excited with vainglory and desolation. In between the prayers Father Gregory and his assistants broke the pretense of the demon to be as one with Amanda. Father believed that it was a devil's incantations inducing the demon to take possession. To know the name of the demon was not an easy task for them. After an abusive crescendo, horrible panic, worst type of other worldly smell and frightful babel at the very breakpoint they got to know the identity of the demon and how it entered the body. Father Gregory had to undergo tremendous physical and spiritual pressure, placing his life in great danger. He got to know the entity's name but he never disclosed it. The demon revealed an address confessing that he lived with someone in unit 213 of the Oxford Apartments at 924 N. 25th Street, Milwaukee, Wisconsin.

In the great triumph of God's will and in the name of Jesus, the demon left Amanda and she was reclaimed. But after that she became a complete lunatic, wanting to eat human flesh, begging everyone to take her to Lionel. Liam remembered that Amanda told him that as a teen she used to brood over the possibilities of cannibalism. And he jokingly replied- "You should have tried to have Anorexia under the circumstances, Amanda". Liam regretted if only he had known it that time, he would have helped her.

Amanda had to go back to her home at Wisconsin in September, 2008. It was painful for Liam to say Goodbye to her. She had no choice but to leave Australia in order to admit herself in Mendota Mental Health Institute in Madison, Wisconsin as a patient of the Windigo Psychosis Disorder, a disorder which was marked by the desire to eat human flesh. Oddly enough during the time of her admission in the hospital, Amanda had no memory of the ordeal she went through in Australia.

Liam and Amanda never met after that. Their love affair was forged in the crucible of a spiritual battle. Liam quit his job as a school teacher in the US and decided to stay in Brisbane with his dad.

Liam still wondered about the mystery of the address given by the demon to Father Gregory as it was the address of the notorious serial killer Jeffrey Dahmer's home. The mystery remained why Amanda in her utter insanity desperately wanted to go to Lionel. Was it the middle name of Jeffrey Dahmer she referred to? Ironically both Jeffrey Dahmer and Amanda Merchant's birthday was on May 21. Dahmer's birth year was 1960 and Amanda's 1990 as if the number 6 in the year had wickedly changed its position by being upside down, Liam thought. Liam wished he could solve the puzzles of this world. Being mazed in total despair, he felt that this world was full of cannibals that we didn't even know or notice. All he ever knew was that the end time was never far away...

Unsheltered

It's quarter past two in the morning and he is still sleepless, completely wakeful. This sleeplessness is not because of insomnia; but some incurable thoughts like a disease are behind this.

<u>Mbizo Chirasha</u>, the great Zimbabwean poet, author and social activist, won't blame his mind for being restless in bed. He wishes his tiny bed and the width of the sky could be in close vicinity. He knows, fate resolves to determine his whereabouts. He couldn't sleep as though slumber land has become a forbidden place for him, ever since he left his own mother land.

His heart aches for his home and his mind is constantly haunted by all the negativity of an insecure life. But he has no choice. He never had a choice, when all he ever wanted is the best for his countrymen. To save his precious life he is now living a life of an unknown existence in a foreign territory. And his strength is losing its shine like an abandoned sword after a vanquished battle.

Throughout the night he has been ransacking his memories in a quest for a little contentment and there somehow, he is able to find so many events and wonderful achievements of a life worth living. Closing his eyes he can see it all; yes, he feels it all- how he worked with many organizations as a creative interventionist, as a performing poet in NGOs, in the United Nations and National Galas; how he served peacefully!

He smiles by himself recalling all those beautiful days in his country when he initiated and worked on a series of projects motivating, educating and developing the Zimbabwean youth. He knows people love him because he touched many hearts filled with youthful vigour through his thought provoking writings on various themes of life, reformation and vitality. He loves those glorious days when he cooperated with grassroots initiatives, foreign organizations, 100 Thousand Poets for Change, the UN, the US embassy's cultural section and the Goethe Centre to bring good things to his own country, Zimbabwe.

He can never forget how people used to inspire his great deeds by saying – "Mbizo, you are a blessing to this world. Never give up, this world needs you." So he went on and still goes on working for the glaze of truth. He wants to spread the gentle sheen of light reforming darkness. His writing seeks political justice in his own country. He knows that his work reveals the truth and corruption of society which includes the current political situation in Zimbabwe. But he never wants to hold himself back.

At the same time Mbizo's mind feels heavy now with the fatal burden of patriotism. But deep down inside he loves to bear this load of love for his own soil. The dark force of his country has been trying to drag the love out of his patriotic heart, the heart that beats only to make this world a better place.

As he is tossing and turning in bed, all those titles of his well known poems: Dear Mother, Haiti, Haiti, Haiti, Dream Of Rain, Diary of the Povo, Forty years after dawn, Kalinga- linga, Children of Xenophobia, Black Oranges, Blue Lemons are echoing in his mind.

Suddenly a horrid memory comes to plague him again. It was midnight, he recalls, when a car pulled into the yard of the house he used to live in. The car doors were banged hard in order to draw attention. During that time he was the only guy in that house and the oldest one. In about few minutes the car drove away. After an hour the car came back and continued to bang doors like before.

He still remembers, he didn't go out to see. He heard people talking, mentioning his name. Instantly the car pulled away again. Later that night he fell asleep. He remembers, he woke up by 1.30am in a scary electrical shock. His spine still shivers in an eerie coldness, remembering how he was perspiring and struggling to breathe after that tremendous shock. Even his pillow felt like it was electrocuted. His head was completely numb. He peeped out of the window and saw people with torches, talking on their cell phones. He spent the night in terror waiting for the morning light to arrive to rescue him. Now he knows, it was a tool called Guntezza which was used for electric shock, perhaps for disabling or for kidnapping him or maybe to send him to the other side. He had to leave that place in search of his life's security.

Soon after the Literature Festival of 2017, threats and attacks began to chase him everywhere. He still doesn't regret that he has been very quiet after the first attack because by nature he is always a peaceful person. But as days pass by, situations have become unbearably insufferable. He even has no clue who those people are chasing him to take his life away. He can only sense they are the oppressors from his country who hate to let a brave voice speak the truth. So they want his life from him as if the call of the dark needs to be answered by a real patriot's soul. Yes, they want him to be dead anyhow.

He thinks about that mid-January of 2017 when he relocated to another place where he received phone calls from strangers, wanting to see him without disclosing their identities. He still wonders why he didn't care about those mysterious phone calls initially.

He can still go back to January 22, 2017 in his mind when three men, who appeared to be overly investigative, approached him in various locations in Harare. He found them stalking him in so many places he went. Now he thanks the Lord that he evaded them so that they wouldn't get him.

Mbizo cannot get January 24, 2017 out of his head as he clearly recalls how a man wearing security guard gear was lying in wait by the tree near the room where he stayed with a friend in one of the leafy suburbs of Harare. And yes indeed, to attack him again that hidden man was there. Mbizo had to leave that place as well since he kept on hiding himself from places they chased him.

He is in constant mental affliction now realizing the fact that his life has lost its deserved place in his own country. One question keeps on returning to his conscience is why he had to carry on changing his location in his own city…in his own country?

On January 26, while in another location, he understood that he was being tracked because the people he was staying with found an unknown man at midnight leaning on the window of the room he was sleeping in. And like the other strangers, he too fled and disappeared into the blackness of night when people saw him. And on February 3, 2017 Mbizo was stalked again while having a drink at a restaurant, the stalkers this time pretending to be policemen when they were not.

Mbizo still remembers every single incident. He doesn't know what or how to name them- Stalkers? Incognitos? or Predators? Each of their unidentified existence disconcerted him, scared him beyond his unquestionable brevity. He remembers while going to the station how he was so flamboyantly followed by a white car that came right by his side. By God's grace he in some way managed to get home that night.

But the next day, February 4, 2017, he decided to leave…only because he had to. Throughout the night he walked around, looking for his own security in the country he was very securely born in, the country where he spent his wonderful childhood, the country he worked for throughout his meaningful life.

Closing his eyes again Mbizo visualizes all the things he used to do in his homeland – gardening, housekeeping, child minding, farming, teaching, writing, creating verses, performing poetry…so many things that he dreams to do again in his own land. But the cruelty of reality makes dreams unreachable.

Those life threatening menaces seem to never leave him alone. Mbizo is now spending his sleepless nights under various roofs of foreign countries: from Zimbabwe to Zambia …from South Africa to Swaziland to Lesotho…from Lesotho to…somewhere else…under the same African Sun he has been taking shelter. Perhaps a nomadic Bedouin used to live a stable life more secured in the burnt desert. He feels that to rescue his own life he has to stay in a safe place; doesn't matter if it is on Planet Mars or in a beautiful tree house somewhere in this world.

Staring at the ceiling Mbizo realizes that he needs to sleep as the clock ticks on and his exhausted eyes squint to read – 3:45am.

Drifting away he suddenly remembers a line he read somewhere…

"The land is always there…it is you who has to return."

(Inspired by the real life of the great Zimbabwean poet/author in exile Mbizo Chirasha. This story previously published in TUCK MAGAZINE - Political, human rights and arts magazine from Canada; Publication date: July 7, 2017)

The Half Circle

The Bougainvillea tree has been enjoying its own blossoms since the beginning of spring. These thorny ornamental vines are everywhere in Dhaka. Almost all the residential houses have one or two of them decorating the lifeless brick buildings or walls.

Arif, the 9 year old street child occasionally like to sit on one of those footpaths where the purple bracts of waxy Bougainvillea are carried by the wind from a house nearby. He looks at the tree, a few steps away, and wishes to be a sepal still attached to the cluster of three flowers - at least in that way he feels the security of a family bond. Arif loves bougainvillea so much but he doesn't know that they are incomplete flowers without corolla. They don't have petals, only colorful modified leaves. And sometimes those leaves (like many newly-rich people in this city) are so highly modified that the veins seem nonexistent or don't look like veins at all.

When bougainvillea's flower dries up, it shrivels and a dry fruit appears. But Arif does not need to know all this botanical detail - too much of information for him. Arif's nine year old life has gone so dried up already with poverty's scorching heat, but perhaps a fruit will come up.

This area full of bougainvilleas is 2 and half miles always from Arif's living place. Arif lives with his mother's brother in a drearily drab slum where mosquitoes want to make friends with him every night after he sleeps. His uncle, Rahim is a street cleaner who collects garbage using a shovel and broom every day from 5am till night. The fact never bothered Rahim's mind that when it comes to 'earning money for survival', dirty garbage on the street can become so valuable to one's life.

Arif misses his mother who died of cholera three years ago. His father disappeared when he was two and Arif was never enlightened about what happened to him. He doesn't even know, if he is an orphan or not, since there's no news of his father's death- only tracelessness. His new life without parents has always been a burden to his uncle who came to Dhaka only because there's no source of income in the village he was born in. But poverty has never stolen his heart of gold and he loves his nephew very much. This 23-year-old sweeper brought his nephew to Dhaka in hope of their survival. Perhaps, Arif could earn some money soon.

The man who hired Rahim is a kind gentleman. One day Rahim decided to ask him for a job for Arif. And eventually after an interview with Arif and days of begging, he managed to convince him to hire Arif as a child cleaner.

'Thank you so much, Sir. God bless you', Rahim thanked his boss.

'How can I ever repay your kindness. Thank you', Rahim further added.

Arif will be paid US$6 per month for collecting garbage. Happy tears start running down Rahim's sun-burnt cheeks and he could hardly wait giving the good news to Arif. He doesn't know that child labour is a severe crime. All he knows that he wants his loving nephew to be his earning partner so that they could eat food together and live.

That night Arif returned his uncle's place walking and running two and half miles from that area filled with bougainvillea trees. It was around 8pm when he entered into the slum discovering his uncle fried two eggs after a long time for dinner. Egg is Arif's favorite food. So, he became so delighted. He ate it with Rahim mixing with steamed rice.

"Arif, you will start working from tomorrow, okay?", Rahim said after finishing his dinner.

"Really?", Arif's wonderful black eyes sparkle with a joyful surprise.

He suddenly stood up and hugged Rahim.

"They will teach you how to clean garbage tomorrow using the shovel", said Rahim.

"You will love it." he added.

"You are the best, Mamu" Arif replied hugging his uncle so tight to his chest.

Merry excitement thrilled Arif so much that he couldn't even sleep. He seemed to have started to love the mosquitoes tonight allowing them to suck and drink his blood. His thin brown body was so relaxed believing his little dream of earning money would become true tomorrow morning. Arif fell asleep finally. And the tiny half circle of the crescent moon outside the slum gave him no hint whether it was early in its first quarter or late in its last quarter. The moon knew that Arif didn't need to know all this detail. It only left the hope for a full moon illuminated by the sun.

---

www.ingramcontent.com/pod-product-compliance
Lightning Source LLC
Chambersburg PA
CBHW020542080526
44583CB00013B/950